ON THE EDGE OF A MIRROR

LEE GOLDSTEIN

Volume 2 (3rd edition)

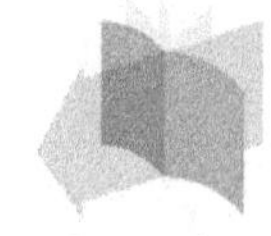

Chapbook Press

Schuler Books
2660 28th Street SE
Grand Rapids, MI 49512
(616) 942-7330
www.schulerbooks.com

On the Edge of a Mirror – Volume 2

3rd edition

ISBN 13: 9781957169217

Library of Congress Control Number: 2021919141

Printed in the United States by Chapbook Press.

Table of Contents

Childhood and Family

Childhood

Set apart, I was a sort of a free atom,
and my family knew how to daff
the many perplexed aspects of the world,
or, perhaps, that too much involved me,
and they were not themselves.
When a child,
I knew I was different,
but I became a member of my surround
and discovered myself,
both in the variety and the miscellany of the world,
to be myself
among these adults,
and to suffer of their somethingness and reflexive of themselves,
as they were styled,
and displayed in the normality of being.

Father (I)

"You can win at home only up to a certain point,
that is, until we become jealous,"
up to an *examinational labyrinth in white:*
This game you may win elsewhere,
with information about rules withheld
and with whose anxiety
in which you are set on a high-brow course,
or it being defective.
Yet whose nominalism of that course
would still favor us.

The Son

The *necessity* of the son
is the *father* inventing space for him
by the father's spirit.
For the son flew over that which it lacked
and the family accepted him that way
at the emotional school of hard knocks,
where they regularly tried
to render him so unmanifest in this world,
or formerly moved to push him so far ahead.

Father (II)

In one's heartiness
is a transparency
or a story of morals?
In some ways, the father
was a mime
of the pursuit of happiness,
his success like the winning
of so current of
intelligence games.

Negative Anecdote

Having a social worker in the brother,
made me a better laughing stock-
to practice within the family
what you have been ethically warned
not to do.
And when at the dinner table in 1986,
mother, sitting stolidly through
the whole scene,
or as systemless,
didn't turn her head,
while I said something normal,
(a nearly direct quote of my rabbi, no less),
and the social worker responded to my apparently
egregious false guise
by a laugh, briefly, heinously,
in a bizarre way
to my face,
as a kind of provocative therapy:
The impromptu gig
had me freaked
for a short time,
to remind me, to press me,
in the true belief of his,
that I could never, really, bespeak normalcy,
which I just putatively appeared to do.
Rather, my essence as insanity and rot to him,
and at the very least,
I was more predictable to act
like the latter.
And mother never turned her head,
and having been as good and effective this once,
the gambit should surely
succeed a second or third time, and so on,
or of that mainstream of society,

its sentiments, as they are,
toward the workless.
That's it!:
The brother could write a book to defend himself and exalt his
success,
his beliefs and techniques,
his Draconian ways,
perhaps, calling it (and with intentions, as they are),
after the Beatles' song, be as liberally,
"Maxwell's Silver Hammer".

A Family

The family had sometimes
believed itself self-made,
or perhaps, group-made,
save my mother
in her later years:
They believed in the right
of the pursuit of happiness,
and Old World social mores –
That was confusing for my mother.

My parents had
a basic put-up-manship
toward us.
But I, the second born,
was nevertheless
early, 'particularized'
in the family,
or even like
a bound-down individual.

I seem to have been raised,
somewhere between
a 'put-up-with'
and a 'put-down',
though the above
was reconciled
by an education,
or so intent,
in which I was encouraged.

Carl

1976, in Dr. Carl Whitaker's office in Madison:
I, soon to begin my graduate studies in Ann Arbor,
the ensemble of my family who did not want
to take on my
karma to themselves,
practically speaking,
nor was I accepted
as a 'social concept'
to the rest of the family.

My family, now sans the father,
did not care
for my 'alternate knowledge',
nor that of Carl's:
That we ought to be in essence, together,
or, otherwise, leave them alone,
for they were at this time
just as dutiful to me
and cordial to Carl.

Sibling Rivalry

The older brother
ought to assume a place
to be the guardian
over the younger brother
in order to protect
from many *other* relationships--
His practice of discouragement
and that of those associations
onto the younger brother.

The older sibling wants to connive
a projection
from an otherwise positive acquaintance
to me, exactly,
or the same way
he had wanted of our parents' relation to me,
or to be the inferior one
unto them
of me.

In a kind of embarrassment
to the family,
the older sibling
should oblige himself
to be
a negative 'fixer'
to the younger 'unfit',
or an undeserving one
of his divers privileges.

And he should bully
to rule over the picture
of a family's interpersonalness.
Or in the way,
he could determine himself
to be the family's winner
and a family system
that can be rejected,
who be in the younger one.

Family Anxiety

He, who in practice,
will not do anything
that does not,
as a modus operandi,
disilluminate himself,
or the bullied one
similar to the 'fourth leg'
of a perennial would-be
three-legged stool, being like the family.

A family anxiety
could be like
a denial of
the fourth leg
in a three-legged stool,
or that is
the family's
to which would-be being
a fourth leg as perennial.

The family would sometimes
only cite three people
of the family,
or denying
the fourth member,
to thieve
an intellectual property,
that could make, as much of things,
all the more difficult.

Exertion

My family, sometimes,
seemed to 'silly'
or negate
my intelligent exertions,
or as if
to hinder,
or even to disaffect
of my deficits,
that for my future's own good.

Dominion

He seeks to be in relational control of others, having started with
his father before me,
and it is true that, in my infancy,
he was relationally stimulating to me,
but soon he sought to have this situation altered,
when he surmised that in controlling me
required that I be left in disrelation,
for nowadays, he wants
to boss every positive relation associated with me out,
in order to drive me mad,
and once mad, to him, I am conquered.

The Negligible Son

To be what you are to yourself
and to privilege, to complement, to encourage yourself,
as you see fit,
even to have a few atypical friends
to honor you –
But unto us, your nuclear family,
it remains that
this is our home
and you are our ignoramus.

House in Chicago

I must have contributed little, all considered,
or to have *purloined* my parent's house (!),
to grow up in from the time of my infancy,
being conferred there
all enjoyments and privileges
of being a member of my family.
Yet, save, I later must be made
to feel ashamed for the earlier *theft* in my existence,
which for having been born to my family.

Mother

Women, of whom the most natural,
tend to be the stewards
of social relationships.
More than my mother's generosity
in her resources to me
of making our household
ever safe to live or visit,
was of her exquisite relationalities,
or, alas, yet as conditional.

Family System

Mother was unpredictable
of having burst her sometimes general resentments on us:
The brother's agenda
was the transference
of the part of shame from him onto me,
or he was
ever to put me down
from after the time of my infancy
to the present.

System

A child to his parents or adult acquaintances
could be models for his own behavior,
if there should be an emotional void from his family:
Otherwise, would be his "trainers".
Yet whom their neuroses of their own behavior--
its passage unto the youngster's own,
or in some circumstances,
their modus vivendi could be the passaging
onto the fomentation of the infant's own neurosis,
or, in turn, the predisposition of the child's dependency.

Umbilicus

Not all having been of the earliest
spiritual tetheredness
to the mother:
Or could, much later,
the many a doctor's
substitution of this order,
or the relation through time,
for need it yet be
a chemical etiology?

On Being Born

In the dawning
of my birth,
after the Second World War-
Soon upon me,
on the other hand,
was the sort of
overly personable insensibility,
whereof the many social styles-
And have a nurture of the unnurtured.

Caveat

There may also be
a kind
of imparticibleness,
or unsharedness,
in space,
instead, the less of
whose original
contact with
the mother.

A Noncontributory Son

His mother and father
privileged their son's development of his talents
in their large house
and yet did not encourage
his talent's outright relations toward the world, at large,
and where he should not compete with the parents,
even unto the future,
to remark their own liberality,
and right in front of him.

Atypical Parenting

To view a parenting
and say nothing of it:
Or what objectification
of the infant
to precede an empathy for him or her:
If the family will not set a space
for the infant,
then the infant must set a space
for the family.

Early Family

Earlier, of the infant,
and in the sight of
a person's demeanor, too,
may be like a percept
of a 'figure on a pillar'
in another style
and the infantile sentience of people,
or could be that
until a life's rational motility.

And earlier on, my family did not know
what to make of me:
That I was someone who "hangs out",
or seeking those who "hung out",
as free spirits,
or if the likes of a gypsy,
who has his own story,
and be free in laissez-faire.

The family's sense of not knowing what to make of me,
when I was small,
was a kind of not caring about those who are too *crazy*--
Or to be weakened in interpersonal ways:
Therefore, to be conscionable,
by an effort, or to try again,
unto an ad hoc will
and not over their unconsciousness
in the family.

The Honeymooners

Father and I,
as co-goofy pals?
The brother would simulate this,
wherever I am,
and thereby honor
his father's integrity,
or that when the father's integrity
is synonymous
with the both's success.

Schadenfreude

Not commonized enough
to their minds,
I was made
to pay through the nose
for my early privileges,
my dues for a spite of mediocrity
in which the family attitude
toward me
ought to continue through much of my upraising.

Family Contest

The family chose
from a variety of therapeutic services,
those that were inadvertently
due a rehabilitation
from a would-be professional person in the family,
and effectively, if deciding
to deal with sibling rivalry,
or otherwise, the matter
of competing smarts, et. al. in the family.

The Contestation

The accusation of myself,
"tapping the vital sap," so to speak,
or socially,
an intent
to do anything possible
to make me
look unprofessional –
Or that should answer
to his rivalry with me.

Nugatory

In the youth's course, real or figurative,
"of throwing money" at him,
instead of having gotten
the personal encouragement
for his future prospects
or lest the belief in him
for his later life's trade –
He is anticipated, rather, to tarry
in the proper prerequisites
for what profitability of work,
when the best is to flourish,
but having been handicapped, as such,
or, as so, for his future's own good.

Dégagé Family

The how of my family seeing me
was as *de facto* insignificant,
or inestimable to them,
to attain
for themselves
a *de jure* respect,
or be *soi-disant,*
was their attitude
to me.

Idiosyncrasy

He is an idiosyncrasy,
ruled by the personal in him,
when in his ambience
nothing might signify
outside him, save a liberty in arbitrariness
towards him.
And may he no longer have any higher privileges –
Like a child,
or aught on whither whim, we can all now stop caring.

Family (I)

You ought to treat people of your own family as "points of light"
and not pooh-pooh them,
for we all need such ministrations
in the families of the world,
or if one truly stands alone: Is it possible?
And if amongst one's family,
one may look like a point of light,
he or she *is* a point of light.
But guard oneself against an external *deceit*.

Family (II)

A break from an aboriginal culture in Russia,
where one perennially
had to do what one elsewhere was not able
to do for the best of one another,
or because they had no abundance.
And our own privilege in America
from the father's new-found success in a chosen profession
or that of the consequences in the above attitude,
when the present day family believes somewhat in the *disregard* or
the *unconcern,* per se, in the former
at the new sort of freedom to be able to
pay more attention to the wants and the dislikes of their own,
than be so obliged to the rules, as egregiously,
of the other people's laws, above us.

With the rights in this country
in its pursuit of happiness
is an alternative
by what obligations
in sometimes uncouth an interpersonalness
of families in the old country–
Yet, here a *laissez-faire,*
and in its intercommunications–
Instead of another's sequesteredness in duty.

Family (III)

A "zero-concept" family:
We are all autonomies
outside of one-another,
unrelated and free:
This means we can dream up
the most of ourselves
in a future of societal merit:
And that the family might rebuff
such needs of one each other.

Family (IV)

Of my family,
or I being as foolish to them-
And in our dialogues,
or our absence of dialogues-
And at their behest,
my chores done,
and perennially, too,
they might leave me abroach,
or in a want of empathy.

Family (V)

Of one's behavior,
cited in sorts
of one's family,
thereupon, that very behavior,
at large,
of the above
is not good
for seeing one another
of their essence.

Family (VI)

My family, or like such a constructive modus operandi:
We were generous to each other,
without necessarily
believing in believing in one another:
And in an integrity,
we should be like the picture of ourselves,
pulling ourselves up
by our own boot-straps-
Or to be the best.

Family (VII)

My family was much like
the would-be befooling of an anti-Semitism,
after the massive jeopardy of events in Europe--
Or our behaviors being averse
to each other?
That is, to be the compensation
of sorts--
Or, therefore, the competition, too,
and our achievements.

Family Therapy

Of the meeting with Carl (1976)
for our session
of family therapy
at his office
in Madison, Wisconsin,
the mother and brother were "normal",
so had an instantaneous communal rapport with Carl,
whereas to me,
Carl, not a professional peer,
would to my own evident family uncommunalness.

Family Unconscious

The family, later, of the older brother,
would not sufficiently put out their time
for interpersonal matters with me.
Soon, the brother would be at liberty
to have rule over latter issues,
and in or out of my family, which could affect
both of my social relations, at large,
and in the outcome of my profession, as an adult,
but lean, as unsure, on what life's common skills.

As an adult,
he grows his spiritual powers
with a kind of
mocking-up, or conserving,
of the family conscious
from the past,
or having been so scourged
in the psychoanalyses,
or by its followers.

Narcissism (III)

My family seems to have
a long history of "inexisting" me, emotionally,
instead of conceptualizing me-
rather, their own itemization
of such personal issues,
to lessen
the consequent stress and strain
of living-
And the external world.

Repellent

43

I should seem to be charged
by my family
in the blame,
for my own
infant's *disdain* of my family,
or their would-be
inattention to me,
or both behaviors above
are equal and opposite.

To cajole
the disfavor
of my family origins
onto the present,
unto the acquaintance of associations,
and of friendships
to others, at large,
to enter in society,
but poorly be done.

Genetic Ridiculousness

A neo-Nazi, whom I recently heard speak,
denied the holocaust,
saying this (supposed) event
was "ridiculous".
Similarly, the sibling, (or 'Big Brother')
had for many years seen only his younger brother
as a "silly person",
if not as ridiculous
in what he says and does,
while a sillying person
may tend to see the world and to everyone else as silly,
and be, too, the older brother, defending himself from him.

Our family, also, posited
the kind of a
genetic 'goofiness'
of the family
that was saved
by our grace
in otherwise,
or if so consequentially,
what the nonexistence of God.

Family Idyll

My family believed it had
the right of no response, socially,
and save of itself
the fashionable,
the conformable,
or even driven,
by mental pictures
in their prospects
and of life's promise.

Father (III)

My father tried to
stave off Hitler's shadow
from our family,
after the war in Europe.
And in America,
this was done
through his 'game theory'
in the acquisition of monies in life
and his focus on the intelligence.

Father (IV)

With the father was the winning capital,
(or means of production),
in setting up a laissez-faire home economy.
Yet, too, a manner of contestation that continues to this day
is the older brother taking on the winning capital,
that the father might not so have such a social ethic to stop–
And the younger brother having a losing capital,
the older brother's own bullying provocations,
or is the younger brother's pretense in suppositions.

Father (V)

After my father's passing
in the Fall of 1971,
I could garner
no likely
social concept
of myself
from the mother,
the brother,
or of the remaining family.

An Early System

Of his infantile years
from his family,
or even
a familial tackiness,
who, particularly, is
the younger child,
not so much
by the autonomy,
or to be as extreme a system.

Personable

To be over-personable,
yet to an infant:
Or, otherwise, to set
in a field of being-
And in lieu of
life's concepts' space-
Of creating a sort of
being, or the slowing
of this, an otherwise maturing child.

Family Legacy

An intense ignorement, or inadvertency,
was the family's
sometimes strategy
to cut through
a society's anti-Semitism,
by the achieving of the
appropriate hard-line a focus on whatsoever tasks
to become a success in the profession and the head of the family,
and after of what conclusion of the Second World War.

Synchysis

In being raised by my upper-middle class family,
there did not seem all that much a concerted effort
to interpersonally communicate with me
past my own infant's synchysis to them.
And the envy of the family
would leave my precocity a hodgepodge--
And when the older brother began school,
he left me off, and in no further a good faith to stop trying to
understand me--
and pursue his own bullying ambitions,
my otherwise waxing brightness
left me to be disabled, and, again, to my own self's confusion.

Shetl

In my Jewish American family,
still the shetl *antics,*
in attitudes and behaviors
inherited of our lineage
from Eastern Europe,
(even to us, second-generation Americans),
to remain now necessary,
or to protect ourselves
from such prejudices.

An Early Family

Our early family,
and thereon
to mock
my interpersonal control,
or act like a fool
to appease the gentiles,
as in a shetl,
in the outcome, later,
or like a poor listener.

An American Judaism

Earlier generations of Jews
in the cities of America
near the turn of the 20th century,
having come from the old country,
can, too, be a people,
who have a neurotic interpersonalness,
like their social /business of free expression in this country,
having cited their new found rights
of the pursuit of happiness.

America

To cite my ancestors coming to America
from Eastern Europe
at the turn of the 20th century,
hitherto, there had been no specific pursuit of happiness
principle,
nor an allowed ownership of property.
And in their modern fate in America,
there may sometimes be a difference
between intrinsic heartiness in the pursuit of happiness,
or the outcome, too, of one's better character—or not.

Aging

Senior

If a lull in dignity,
being an older person,
or monotonous in time:
You are chided, of course,
of their only possible regimen here,
and they will force you
to like it,
whether you adopt it now as an attitude,
or not.

Senior Residence

Many residents of senior housing
practiced a passionate "neglecto-philia"
over my various and studious labors,
or when I worked in the commons room,
I was accused of taking advantage
in a privilege –
I was supposedly usurping others' social space.
The many simple retirees, there –
Retirees from the stresses of the world,
being apparently easy victims
of my furious "quid pro quo", so said,
a program taken,
instead of others' easy comfort,
my wanton expropriations in writing
are simplified an accusation in the writer.

Senior Place Blues

Residents of Rockhill Senior Apartments
are largely enticed
into strung-out dreaming
of illusory non-defeat
before their retirement.
And they are yet winners,
because they have won over the nothingness
by keeping themselves as busy, as occupied,
for the latter part of our days.

Old Folk (I)

Older people need dignity and sustenance.
Yet there is a perennial caveat in old folk,
who become aware of themselves
of their special conforming
in the prevalence in their ages,
or, annually, have a significance,
less the substance, or a killing of time,
and in their communications
among each other.

Old Folk (II)

Old folks,
in a last resort,
to push
the river
of time –
Or ruling time
and to own
the very space
of their surround.

Old Folk (III)

Notwithstanding, many older people,
who at work into their elder years
claim, "I am 'ergophiliac'.
Therefore, I exist".
Or to many people, excessively as dilute
of the many's love in their sentiment
the muse says, "I want to rule
over the raffle
in a field of love."

Old Folk (IV)

Such a community
of ergophobic older people
can be
more attracted
in regular visits
to the doctor's office,
because the latter
has a milieu of ergophilia,
or is just for them.

Old Folk (V)

A challenge for groups of older folks:
To bear their complaints
in so much blather,
like a people's people, or if a pattering,
or in the pursuit of happiness:
Then to make an ongoing gamble, one to another,
the convention out of an unknown,
when it is only the few alive who know
what their bodies are doing to them.

Old Folk (VI)

After living with old folk
for a number of years in senior housing,
he complains about the waning of
a passion living there,
or which lessens
his generality of a personal value to other people
with his general sequesteredness
and further limiting
in the span of human possibilities.

Old Folk (VII)

Leaving off such provisions
for their private selves,
having been responsible people
during their working lives,
is not deserving
of the burden of estrangement
in their later life,
lest we reach leaving off the forbearance,
or lean as much on alter social ends.

Old Folk (VIII)

Any longer, no work done to *relate* to us, as such:
Just a nominalism
of our being an a posteriori,
socio-spiritually *relatedness* to,
because the first is deserved
by their senior social class,
or their retirement
in whose past's respectful labors
and the elder citizens, now.

Old Folk (IX)

Later, in a term
of retired living,
or be like
who might sunder,
or a laxity
in whose mental concentration span:
And the second
was obliged
of his working life.

Old Folk (X)

Old folk, of various and sundry
so infirmity,
might also entail
this group
of would-be individuals,
sitting in the doctor's waiting room:
Those of whom
are only per a proxy
of the doctor.

Old Folk (XI)

A continued concern to exhibit
better mannerisms in society
is not only the matter, at large,
for being civil,
but, again, *to think–*
Can be believed
by many old folk
to lend themselves
of less which good manners.

Old Folk (XII)

Of the professional employees,
who have suppressed their needs by necessity
due to the demands on the workers
in their terms of employment:
When they retire,
they have earned
the interest of those needs be now met and unmet,
or from the Social Security System of state,
and become what voracity of their purpose.

Old Folk (XIII)

Many of the tenants
of Rockhill Senior Housing,
and for the most part,
to be prolix,
or not much
of the practice of
a linguistic individuation,
yet most to insist,
or practice a prate of the speech.

Old Folk (XIV)

To live with one hundred other residents
at Rockhill Senior Housing,
of whom mostly a group with low concentration spans,
or with myself as culpable,
a "hanging out",
rather than
who I honestly ought
to be more individuating
than socializing,
or mete without it.

Old Folk (XV)

Sometimes, to maintain a hopeful rationale,
even a dignity
of the old folk,
as they are–
To a life force,
or through their social pressures
and make-believe,
or whose so far-fetched
in their gambols.

Old Folk (XVI)

In the aged, or the chronically infirm,
of whom there could
be a lost diligence,
or must so instead
of being productive –
Per their very unproductivity:
Therefore, a would-be of this productivity
is doubted
or frowned upon.

Old Folk (XVII)

In social remembrances
of bits and pieces of social patency,
a chortling compassion
in the elders' conversations
with each other
could be thought
to lead them
and pretend
only in a personal illumination.

Old Folk (XVIII)

Sometimes, a plan
to oversee the ignorance
in groups
of old folk,
who, otherwise,
by and by,
would have to confront
more of the naughty events
of themselves.

Self-Responsibility

Resident of Rockhill Senior Apartments:
Carry thy mop,
for thine own feet
might track in the mire
from outside
and onto the floor, beneath one,
or thereabouts,
and here be to one a co-dependency
on thine own building's janitor!

Hysteria

Rockhill Senior Apartments
is government subsidized housing for the retired.
Is it?
Or is it a verifiable "namby-pamby-ocracy",
this contention of one more would-be
false power,
that is trying to make a veritable rule by its own cadgers
in these hard times of our country?
Call in the National Guard!

Folksy

The only knowledge
acceptable here
is folksy,
or cliquish,
by its very nature,
and against *much* knowledge,
this being a popular social routine
that could evade time's despair
at Rockhill Senior Apartments.

Ageism

82

"I can't do
anything practical anymore, myself,
or I am not doing it!"
Thence, I can become
part of the
"thievery's association"
of items –
I, who, myself, reside
at Rockhill Senior Apartments.

Words (V)

83

Words, or when
the gestalts,
can also
tend to be
like *cut-ups*
for the elders of age.
Or words can be
like the emblems
of a losing of willpower.

Hobson's Choice

In the clinic, the doctor
proffers Hobson's choice, saying,
"Either you accept our terms
by being here, as part of the clinical body,
or you can find somewhere else."
Indeed, if a person, on seeing so many doctors
could become a clinical entity,
then what desire, or life's love
of the clinical object?
For this is the way we should have
it set up for him,
of being let by the managers of his current residence
at Rockhill Senior Apartments.

Hobson's choice: the choice of taking what is offered—or nothing

Less Rights

The devil, having been denied his claim to equal rights,
thus, the skimmed rights
in old age, or the infirm,
who are not expected to have such civic rights amidst society.
Or, sometimes, those who are testy
may not bear the pity on some others' presence.
Or, as devilish, in old age, or the infirm:
Those with the more aid,
but still be less the plenum of rights.

A Provincial Writer

Most people of a senior resident housing,
in particular, have the less of themselves
to speak to all of the world.
To exclude myself, the author,
in that atmosphere,
I must be a *red herring*,
to speak to me,
amongst them,
or be "Doctor Red Herring."

Lost

In being lost, the person can be more honest
than in a spurious productivity.
And I should
surrender to an old age,
or the happenstance
of being lost—or that a cynical outcome:
It is understood, that in your being lost
in old age, generally,
on not being productive.

Obligee

In the environ of a senior housing,
others could be obliged
to care about one another.
Therefore, as "In Rome,
do what the Romans do"--
But, at large,
many others' behavior
is either 'toward' another,
or taken aback.

Phantom

89

I have a brain, so to speak,
and, socially, amongst the group
of old folk
in my residential place,
who might, apparently, have less
therein, to see me,
or as a phantomy,
and this is what I should exhort
from where I am.

Evolution and Devolution

Perhaps, one of a later age
and under a bent of stress
at the self's threshold of nonbeing,
motions of the living body,
whose tremulous voice speaks
the distensions of himself
to be like short shrift,
to explicate himself,
as vanity, perhaps,
or liable to be shrived
by the universe
and so his own inertia
by God,
or death,
for being rent of his basic reflections,
being dis-toned,
or a deprival of motion,
and allowed to shrivel:
This is in evolution and devolution.

A Damaged Life in Jewish Modernity

Language (or A-voc-atori-ness)

92

It is not certain
whether modern language
confers a life
or a void.
For language, at times,
is like the sword of Damocles,
hanging over one
in such an exigency
of a moment's now.

A Damaged Life

93

Life is a series of communions,
without which
there are only the fantods,
the more consuming of
the life struggle
in the fear,
the more the risk
of an outcome –
Or less the sense of reality.

Concentration Camp

94

To the Jews,
the concentration camps
were an experiment
in the "inadverting" of God.
Or in lieu of God,
the camps outlied
an intent of having
the atmosphere
of Jews' slights –
Or that in Auschwitz,
God became
the reverse whisperer:
And the concentration camps
were devised
to be ergonomically eliminative.

A Jew in the Mirror

Am I being dependent
on your success' ambition
and take whatever
you hand out to me?
For my function:
You are sovereign and I am not.
Truly, you don't longer care about me,
while you demand to overtop me.
Therefore, having your cake and eat it, too?

God

How may one exhort the likely fact
that the universe
does not always precede
with a priority of copies
to explain its order
or purpose
yet is He, at least,
unto portions of Himself
onto us?

The Resets of Society

Clinic (I)

At this clinic, counselors are trained to advance good character in a pat- and madding way,
with the clients' character regarded as at fault.
Then a person, corrected, could putatively cope better in the world
in consequence of her treatment.
But her nonconformist friends, having previously held high hopes for her,
would continue to develop in their kind of social nonconforming.
And they now secretly hate, or even entertain to persecute her,
for she has seemingly waxed into a false consciousness to them.
And now she is fatuous and denatured to them in her adjustments.

Clinic (II)

In the clinic is
a continued accruing
of the imprint of "schizophrenia",
or until it becomes like a behemoth
with the treatment—and the deconstructing
of the behemoth
by confrontation,
notwithstanding the nonstop delusions
of the client.

Clinic (III)

If society is to be
a majority of professionals,
what major factors
of its civility
requires to not have
the blatancy, or splaying
of its idiosyncratic, or motley, social behaviors –
And some of its clients of the clinic are conditioned
to be unprofessionals.

Clinic (IV)

Schizophrenia is better
not all a clinical object.
Or what is
a possible desire
in the clinical passage
for the better, as mentally ill,
than an unprofessional,
when the best
is one in suit and tie?

Clinic (V)

A treatment in a clinic in California in the 1980's
was purposed to be economo-wise.
Its convenient, sundry truths of what is psychological,
and rather with its espoused verificationism,
or unconcerned with the spiritual emergencies
in the want of its operation,
but suitable for a money trail,
else, likely, that not permitted
to practice at all.

Clinic (VI)

Inevitably, to speak of
the evaluation,
or the inseparability,
having been
in practice,
both the 'good and bad'
that could be
much of the clientele
unto their clinic.

Clinic (VII)

Under whosesoever treatment,
a patient can be aided
in a sort of "irreality-free" meritocracy.
Yet his treatment could also be "image-fixing",
through a half-"robotic" positivism to the patient.
Otherwise, in an unwording legend,
the clinicians should have control
of the implicit linguistics,
or owned over the patient.

Clinic (VIII)

The clinic has
a kind of
"lexicographical legend"
for its mental illnesses:
Its 'inorganic spiral'
like a sort
of unwordedness,
and as synchronous
with what is voluntary.

Clinic (IX)

Many professionals at clinics
might redintegrate their patients,
unto such an appearance
of a "mental illness".
Or in one's social circles
pertain to the clinic:
"Why do people leave to your life
without the clinic,
of when they find you have a 'mental illness',
or in one's social circles.

Clinic (X)

Either a confrontation
or a nonassociation:
In the clinic,
to confront a mental aggression,
or not to associate:
What is signified
of a "mentally ill" person,
as an appellation-
Or even as a "mental hooligan".

A Want of Exhortation

So long as the schizophrenia of the mind
is a surplus of social significance
in its valuations:
A story or a drama
in itself--
It cannot
but limit itself
to be clinically
of its own terminology.

Control

"Mental illness", otherwise,
a sort of nosology of terms,
or the response of the patient
reflects his analyst's
need for more control:
Or they both dole out a tyranny of words,
which the analyst believes
to guide him in this way
in that he can aid the patient.

Stigma Clinic

I should be conditioned
to have, at least, a "normed" aberrance-
Or in denial I should be,
too, ailed to know one, or the other, of myself.
Or if "crazy",
to corroborate one's styles,
which to exemplify
in his own
means of social purpose.

Less a Civic Faith

Within society, a manifest
of mental illness
can result
in a loss of civic faith,
or a mental illness may have
more a concern with their
own human condition's time,
or then only afterwards
their civic existence.

Public Illness

The benevolence of society
has a bias toward the client of the clinic--
to proffer on him a better character
in his re-entrance unto society.
And otherwise, if at large,
he needs must have the continued confrontation,
then he ought to be considered ever else to be
the *disruptiveness* of a person in society,
and being too infirm to do his duties.

Schizophrenia as an Impertinence

The clinic promises its clients
of their own pertinence in the world,
yet not pertinence for some clients,
the illusion from the therapeutic
to promise as beholden to the clients
in their regard.
Yet some clients of more cognizance
can suffer a lingering impertinence,
and the befooling of themselves from themselves.

Limits of an Unindividuated Schizophrenia

As a current working definition of schizophrenia,
or real as a behemoth,
the person concerned ought to be denied
an awe of his own character
for his own tempered good.
And he could be leveled, stabilized,
and prepared for a living in a residential group home
of his choosing after treatment
and a defeat of his delusions.

Impostership in an Average Schizophrenia

His studies at a major university
and his term of work in Research and Development
were none other than a mask of his schizophrenia,
when an avoidant true challenge was but for him to face the latter
squarely in therapy.
And having been given many chances to do that,
he averted opportunities
of not adopting our formalism
to have, as new-fangled a secondary side of himself,
or feign the other's expedient in him, still.

Schizophrenia

Schizophrenia can be a sort of
intention's ampersand:
It is also a psychical configuration
that may have a resolution
per one's specifically personal education.
Or notwithstanding in its internal part
of that illness,
which only a medical doctor,
if at all, can fathom.

The term "schizophrenia"
is a polysemy.
Its appellation to a person
can tend to reduce him or her
from many to one-
And even the misfocus,
with the latter, summarily,
how he or she is seen,
if at all.

A schizophrenic labor,
the durance, or the endurance,
of the illness in one,
is not always the quality
of so much parlance,
nor such an inequitable talk
in a misparlance,
but be through
being as schizophrenogenic.

In schizophrenia,
one can perceive
a cleft world,
or having been, if an infant,
being environed
by the family,
who not knowing,
or pretending
what to make of him.

Subjects of these,
as above,
can also
be opinioned
by others,
or of their being
like a "zero",
or as bad
a life plan.

Killers of the Dream

The therapist is demonstrative of the patient:
"You see, the patient is a sick impostor of his own realism.
And he tries to fool us, perennially:
There is no point in the furthering
of his gain of more a professionalism."
And to ease him unto the general care-giving
in the social systems for that purpose:
What even allows the therapist the right to imagine
he can fathom the patient's dream for himself?

Big Silence

Schizophrenia matters,
but a broken mind doesn't?
To infer
from 'schizophrenics',
the reduction
of terms
to a logocentric conscience?
Epithets for schizophrenia
can go on forever.

The Clinicalization of Ann

Ann, your youthful beauty,
your most prideful quality
puts you on the tally
of respect and desirability.
Yet the guise
belies a turmoil within,
as they treat your illness
of the low
in this guise, and as false, the beauty,
your most prideful quality,
now, clinicalized.
Or needs must that guise being confronted,
when still the borderline case's turmoil.
Ann ought to square with
her own personality's basis,
little that tribute,
to her own grace
in her world
of this affect,
or to mar the beauty,
as inadvertent,
and to send her, again, out into the world
for her own good.
The most prideful quality,
Where, or when it outdoes you
to still follow,
trying to cope in the world,
now to be the underling of the culture's social bosses,
damaged, as you may be
after the treatment,
or no longer fooling the marketplaces of your cities
in this time must be
a co-dependency
for the foreseeable future.

Psychology (I)

We must adopt
to psychological problems of our currency in culture,
because they pertain to us
and in vogue.
Or let the activities we enjoy
be therapeutic, as well:
To have solved our psychological problems
in a primary aim,
or many's modern existence.

Psychology (II)

More than a few psychologists can foment
an echolaliac speaking,
or the sub-vocalizing
of virtual diagnoses
in the client.
And the diagnosticians
tend to make 'fixed images'
of their patient's facets,
rather than the condtions.

Absolute Psychology

When you can't come with me
in another place, even another country,
you behave as though I ought to bear
your selfsame relation to me,
as you had, when you were
here and now to me.
Indeed, you believe your psyche
a law of physics
or for my psychology.

A Clinical Object

To find out that another has a mental illness:
Then they should leave him
from their lives?
Or if the mental illness,
being as the clinical object,
and the object,
not one personable:
From their xenophobia,
still, rather, but a person.

Sophist

Current in today's psychotherapies
is a gabby Protagorean
relativism of the maxim,
"Man is the measure of all things":
Or it becomes to a speech habit of the client,
when the therapist has, perhaps,
been too little conscientious
of his or her responsibilities in the use of language,
or the client as the pupil of a linguistic masochism.

Hearing Voices (I)

It has been said
that what we
don't say
holds the world together.
Yet a jeopardy
of oneself
to oneself
can be
in "hearing voices".

"Hearing voices"
draws from a principle of times,
not the principle
of the rationality of mind,
or which
the only
absolute dominion
over me
is myself.

A Psychologist

He offered me an institutive connection,
based on a benevolence of society
and his management,
where my original family
had been biased in this respect.
He was not particularly on my side
and not so much invested in
my being personally exceptional,
but only until the betterment of character.

Mostly Psychological: a Fable

An abnormality-free nice guy's
subject matter,
and in speech,
is to suppose
the once called
"schizophrenic" person
can synonymize
with him or her
now being cured.

Silly Goof

Do silly goofs have rights?:
Yes, as often enough,
through a moral heteronomy.
Would others have an obligation
to stop-up a silly goof, even as an ignominy?
Should they dispatch a silly goof
through a few acceptant superiors,
or requires his acceptance
by the aforesaid conditioning?

Delusion

In a running quip
of one teasing another:
"There is something on your shoulder."
"What is it?"
"I don't know, but there it goes again!"
The second, too, may be gullible.
And a conservative therapist,
if present,
could call him delusional.

Strangeness

In he who might
evince an unauthoritativeness,
another could
retort to him in an arbitrariness.
And at large,
when the supplication of classes
of the non-criminal, yet under-responsible:
They might be affronted by the noise, too,
Or in the impersonate silence of others.

Mental Illness

Formerly, of mental patients,
were under the regimen of due correctness
to the patterns of their lives,
or have the right
to bed, board, and the interested presence
of caregivers, when at times,
and in their chronicity,
could seem
blemished, or under those circumstances.

For the social stigma
of mental illness
acts as a diminution
of one's self-expression:
And the ideal of the "cure" of mental illness in society,
too, ignores the knowledge of stigmas
that could become like an unprofessionalism-
Or a mental illness
has an unstructurable orthology.

Mental illness most often becomes a *metonymy*
of the patient, or normatively disliked,
or synonymously applied
and stigmatic
in society,
or in the imagination
and on its downside,
or as liable for
a "spiral of insubstantiality."

After such mental states
in which linear expressions,
as equally lateral,
it might follow that mental illness
is like the returned
part of a spiral:
A so-called mental health
of the extension of spirals,
organically, too, schize-ing.

Or, again, mental illness can
have as
unstructurable an orthology,
or an endless synonymy.
Mental illness, too,
can be
like a
sort of
devalued spiral.

Sufferance

In Community Mental Health,
the mentally ill
can be encouraged
to gab about their problems,
under the seniority
of another's ears to lend,
or like a sort of
sufferance granted
to them.

M.I. (Mental Illness)

The worse thing
an otherwise functional person can do
with their mental illness
is to fix himself,
being as a "m.i.",
lest the diagnoses,
themselves, to wreak
an undoing of his functionality
per his own "m.i.".

Of the current state or era,
the "m.i."
can possibly be
like to a malfeasance,
and such conditions
to be regarded
as unproductive–
Or not further as acceptant
in the culture.

To Carl:

By the 1990's,
Carl had dissented from
the whence current mental health field
in Madison, Wisconsin,
in which was to make a conversion of the client
into a *medical illness,*
but with Carl could also be a *dignified story,*
otherwise, or when the mental illness
could be a *clinical object.*

Therapists

Therapists ought to be
trainers for a
healthier psyche.
Yet some therapists
like to out-event
their patients:
And of some psychiatrists:
"Yes, the nosology,
but never the illness."

Causes

A social disapproval,
if one's bad comportment
is preferred
to a repulsion
of the more personal
"mental illness",
as the hierarchy
over what is
the more predominantly not liked.

Crux

An insouciant person,
who could paint
an other's character
to be irrational,
could elicit others
not to care about the latter.
Or that no one
cares about
crazy people.

Unavailed Science

At the beginning of therapy,
some doctors say,
"If this chronic patient does not have me,
then he won't have anyone
any better than me to treat him."
And at the end of therapy,
if baffled,
the unit doctors would say,
"We didn't surmise this outcome."

Stigma and Art

Ought a stigma to be deconstructed,
as an artistic redemption:
And the eccentricity
from the stigma-
For example,
the fittest's survival,
not because of brute-strength,
but a transcending of the stigmatized,
or moral symptomologies, etc.

"Nuts!"

Cite this American scene,
with its culture and commerce
and its populace, as blades of grass,
when popular social and managerial theories
ought better to
aid him, who, as needy to his wellness,
even his capacity, as a patent 'nut',
or ease him into
a proper residential existence.

Bring Back the Psychiatric Institutions

According to the NRA,
in this country of would-be illegal events,
the only way to stop a bad guy with a gun
is a good guy with a gun,
and in the would-be principle
of controlled social events,
the only way to stop a bad schizophrenic,
is the dogged licensed social worker
from a psychiatric institution.

Crazy

He is "too crazy"
to care for
in the sense
that he is
a "psychiatric unconscionability".
And one who cannot
be others' obligee,
if even his return
is barred from normalcy.

A Civil Confrontation

When a speech-act is illegal,
the law might be called in,
or where if by it, others could be put in jeopardy.
And in comparison
to a so-called "speech-schizophrenia,"
the social worker,
in lieu of there being any better social order,
could, as summarily,
be called in to social confrontations.

'Hanging-out' Cure

A new-fangled therapy
can be directed
to the person's
anxiety syndrome
and its cessation
by the aid to a person (s),
or in a protocol,
to "hang-out"
with him.

"Hanging Out"

It can be a grief
in the loss of a social normality,
or an idiosyncratic anxiety,
that can lead to a dependence on the self's *drama, or event:*
It can be believed that a "hanging-out",
with would-be sympathetic others, can be palliative.
But with a gratuitous experience can come out in this "hanging-
out",
or the anxiety of an over-much so experience
may arise, still, and all.

Determination

Being as obvious,
or not so obvious-
Work can be like <u>gold</u>,
or when
the so-called 'therapeutic'
can be *lead*, perhaps,
or in the contrast
of being as
involved in the above.

A Therapist's Agenda

You, as the patient, should be able to lease a reality
from me for the length of time of our sessions
until you can do as well
without me.
Otherwise, you remain
a dependency of being,
less a model dominance
in being as honest of a stead
for self-actualization.

Co-Institutionalism

In a modernity of treatment in the U.S.
for so-called "schizophrenics"
is to be more
societally managed,
now to be *co-institutional,*
at large,
rather than,
as the past,
being *institutionalized.*

Ward (I)

Earlier schools of social work
taught their interns
how to enjoy
the follies of
incorrect behavior
and the unrighteous speech
of a Stygian suchness
in the back wards
of state hospitals.

Ward (II)

It is often not simple
to pride a bill of rights
of people living in whatever
so *imagination* of the back ward of institutions,
or if a malicious formula
to treat a given person
like an institutional personage,
who might relinquish, instead,
his human rights, again, or personal safety.

Descent

The Future of Nominalism

"One day the day will come when the day won't come." (Paul
Virilio).
You could deploy a provocation, (or a hypnopomp),
to recollect the realism from a nominalism,
or heal the well of realism,
for if the day becomes neurotic, false,
and a savage realism left,
to think of it as an emblem of the day,
and not seek too much in the reference of the day,
for it might better be the recognition be left to its own name.

Missing Time

In a modern environ,
people can also be distracted
in their own Post-Modern disability,
or in a missing time--
Thus, less
a productiveness
in their lives,
or unto a forgetting
of the "now".

Another Style

As inconscient, a style of behavior
can be a kind of new-fangledness in an agenda,
a strategy for the general task
that one might intend to be conditional,
or the bearing of a signature of the person,
for the compensation for a task done,
and could be compared, implicitly, to be unconditional,
whose stylization, instead of the absolute,
to the tasked sanctum of a familiarity,
to contrast with a tentative subjectivity vis a vis the tasker,
the latter, extrinsic to the body,
or when a style ought to be contained
in the depiction of the body,
or, again, like a tangentiality to such a descent of the all.

Mooncalf

If the Platonic
idea of reality,
or by a recollection,
is replaced by
the *calving-out:*
To be relative
of a minorating of
the One,
or which makes the world possible.

A Split Subjectivity

My mental disposition at any particular time
is a relative benevolence
of persons in my locale,
who may strain in my situations
and my relations to others,
as a limit of their good will,
who conveys onto me the curtailing
of their positive efforts,
is to cut and serve only closed affairs onto me,
like a "diablerie for the diabolized",
to play into the hands
of those adversarial efforts
to deem what I ought to
already have chosen,
or what I deserve.

Money Gift

I am as ungrateful a person,
or ever was on this occasion
a makeshift figure of a toll bucket before me,
superimposed on me:
That Tim, visiting my town on the east-west toll-road
from the west, stopping here,
when so gracious a due is placed in the toll bucket,
before he and his party
travels onward to their destination in Kansas City.

Superficies

To be in a cooperative,
I am seen, here,
if vapid and shallow:
Therefore, seeming,
as *vapid and shallow-*
And to be
as emotionally,
or to others,
as well.

Derelict

Almost friendless, nowadays, a natural law
for someone who has falsely claimed
the blame in his own parents,
not to have socially bonded,
even in infancy,
yet if truly being his own faulted person,
not theirs:
Of his perennially sick denial
is his modern fate in adulthood.

Shadow

To agonize with him
to him,
who is the preferment,
or to own a control of shadows:
And to have like an analyst's dialogue
is in a shadowing or a branding on the psyche,
when it is better to be responsible
for one not to shadow the other,
or who does not deserve it.

Candles

Language could
hold candles
to the world-
And if not,
one, not conscientious,
could "adust" it,
yet should
"resolve", itself, into
its own references.

adust: to burn to driness

Unobliging

He tried to convince the people,
who I was associated with,
that I was as flaccid
in my social conventions,
or therefore,
one in whom
others were not obliged to,
or others, too,
to defect from the personalities of others.

A Human Concept

Most people in a family, or the community,
can conceptualize one another.
But what of an enclave
that perceives others
through the majority of projections of themselves, as well,
and with common conventions? –
Or that a child can grow up,
as frowned upon,
in the conceit of others in his enclave –
And in their identity.

The Display

A display selects
that one of itself
for power
and sometimes in pictures,
or the grammatical sentences in the language
should be a display.
Yet not necessarily by a brute force,
as the principle of the afore
could pull itself together, and be humane.

What

I am not a quiddity. So what?

In the cause under normal circumstances
of the roof of a house
not falling in is "so what?"
Or should we suffer,
because of the field of many
being as nonchalant
of all manner of things,
or, otherwise, these "stases"
in the world.

They Stoop to Conquer

I, like a territory,
could be won over by others,
if I am rendered raff.
And my potential
is ceded to another, and in their minds,
would extort me in their cadre of egos,
or by their devaluing of being, and even as I shine,
and in which I should try to shrink from myself,
as they stoop to conquer.

Daylight (After Max Richter)

Being a part of bittering,
or to look, perennially, upward,
her steps into the hallway,
and of the fixtures on the ceiling:
Or next to a perception,
across the chasm,
or of a clipping,
and the almost in not yet looking
into the daylight.

Re-picturing

Consider an inorganic spiral
not intersecting its spiral center–
and can be said to be an
"inner ignorement",
rather, as inclusive,
to be a group of people,
and their well-being, as external,
in a re-picturing
of themselves.

Scapegoat

                    171

With one called illumined,
the person he is with
should become illumined, as well–
If the person is fit–
Otherwise, if unfit,
the person can have an arbitrary response to him,
or to indicate
he was as unfit
to begin with.

Temperance

Has the current experience of an era
become like a sundry and miscellaneous
manual for behavior?
Can one's verbosity, ultimately,
be a subduction
in culture?
And does the second become a hindering,
or an expression of what an adduction (or addition)
of temperance?

Deadwood

You had seen to beghost me
and most of your family's desire
was of little further company
with no real explanation,
or you had not realized
your own nonchalant peeling-off
of the friendship,
to have left a raw fruit, exposed,
like to rot on the table,
and when your philosophy, otherwise,
is left disassociated,
or in which you had hitherto
lived, taught, and guided me
for the past decade?

Stir-Crazy on Jupiter

Ought it be to preserve oneself
in these times
of the pandemic–
And to keep a protocol of 'social distance'
between one and another,
to sequester oneself on earth,
or would you rather
be 'stir-crazy'
on Jupiter?

Cult Transference

A positive transference
of all to Him:
Or even another's
rational preferment
to his Self,
be who ought to controvert,
or once again
unto the first
to Himself.

Atypical

For many people,
the sorts of atypicality,
as a difference from the generality
to the norm –
Should not exist?
Or for an unusualness,
even of whose being –
Or in lieu of what being,
yet a kind of fallacy.

The Occult Barber

A barber of the occult-
If 'shaving' and 'clipping'
the inner scalp,
or in whose inner ears,
and the fibrillation
of the cilia
in the subtle movements
that makes the "sound"
of its speech, within.

Hearing Voices (II)

To alternate from
a spiritual agoraphobia,
may be a physical claustrophobia:
Hence, "hearing voices".
And alternating from
a spiritual claustrophobia
can, too, be
a physical agoraphobia,
or what general anxiety.

Magnetic Gifts

An animal beauty can also be in its magnetic gifts,
or that in the hominoid psyche
can be regarded as primitive,
or an 'animal magnetism' that could be ignored (?).
And Neolithic Man in that way could be diminished,
or of the likes of modern man's psychism,
as hominoids having an 'animal magnetism'
disregarded for their aboriginality,
are conditioned, or would not, if to make benign in modern man,
and when in animals acceptable to have them less
regarded as a beauty protected,
or if hominoids, having the spirits of animals,
are therefore suppressed of their primitiveness, as well, and not
necessary the beauty,
or, again, to be as guarded.

Dreamtime

Of a metred time could one not be as reprieved.

The subconscious of one's ilk
may part from a conscious,
or which
to lean or to motion,
on the person's drive,
or leave
the loss of
a time-consciousness–
or of 'missing time'.

Lexicon

Could it be possible,
or at least potential
of the hypothesis
of which
so gainfully
to be explored,
what an ill,
as if lexicalized –
Or, thereby, be to heal?

Panic

My parents came of age
during the Great Depression.
And in their survival,
as held to the uncommon sense in it,
concerning degrees of sanity
in that age of duress,
or to be suggestive of the necessity
of making concessions
to the cares of the world,
in general, and as impersonal.

Defunctive

Conditioning him
to be the otiose core,
as lower of
the practicality
of the intelligence,
or if I depend
too much on others,
I should be inferior--
Or in above be due.

Nonbelief

Beware of the non-belief
in some of the population,
which could be more a personal security
in the "not-caring." Period.
And that the latter could be an easier way,
as a primitivity,
than to take on cared involvements,
of not to grow one another
and the outside personalities:
Or as those beliefs of other ambitions were lies.

The Unbeliever

Psychiatry, by itself, may often not aid
in one's symptomatic 'separation anxiety':
The client then has an ethical life in dependency,
until any of the above's critical threshold,
thereby, if his independence
with what symptomology
he might be dealing with.
And after a relevant entireness of the deficit's configuration
in the client—thereafter, being left, a medical bond.

A Conscient Tragedy

One with a "free identity",
or he, who is relieved
of an ethnically systematic reference:
Yet in racism,
one of a negative express,
may have the bias
against another,
or the latter
being without necessary rights.

One's express in his work
can charge another with an unearnedness,
or the latter like a shade
of an impress of little rights,
like a misregard,
out of what due protection
by common law,
or, when egoically, the autonomy of the former
wells the homonomy of the latter.

Animals

Pets' Care

Despite an arrogant humanity,
we could exercise
such care
of sidling up
to animals (or domestics)
and heal
with them, or by them,
and onto the more peaceful
contingency of our times.

The Cat's Decline

Jim likes his pet cat to have enough yarn to play with,
keeping his yarn, daily, and freely
tossed on the floor, and still refreshed for the cat,
to willingly pay cleaning fees,
so that the cat's yarn should remain clean.
And be things as they are,
he soon could reach the point where his toil of the cleaning
isn't as worth it, anymore, and the yarn disposed of.
Then the cat ought to no longer expect to have her yarn due.

And of Jim, to behave further,
as he had before
toward his cat,
then, liable, the cat, for its nine lives,
might become cloyed
with a sort of 'outside',
in a probability
of the cat's mood's experience
in her mien.

Or a step further
than depicted
in the allegory of 'The Cat's Decline'
of a person or pet,
in an unmeaning,
to incur by the "heteronomy",
a relinquished presence
to its own meaning,
even of its autonomy of motion.

Grace

Young animals don't know malice,
for nurture buoys their joy
in their grace before you:
It is not even the words to save the appearance:
Even the so-called fertile void
can admit of itself,
or as nothing in it is impure –
And by a will becomes the meaning,
and not just the emblem.

Shark

The powers be that bestow their blessings on the shark,
for a shark, outside man,
has been born near supreme.
And a shark "says",
"I'll avail of you, though I don't like you,
for I'll exact every last farthing from you,
for the price of my having suffered my contact with you,
because I am supreme and God loves me,
and I pray every day my thanks to Him."

Propense Words

Words are a bit like your panting pet dog,
now at your feet,
yet under the restraint
of one's required humane treatment.
Your dog, so wanting your acknowledgment of him,
always his enthusiasm for you,
whereas the words, or the semantics,
may have spent out their positive personal design– but not your
dog–
So, if you want a friend, get a dog.

Chimps

A bumbledom for the arts:
It might be observed some chimpanzees cry
when the organ music of J.S. Bach is played.
Would the phenomenon
of these emotions of apes, alone,
have inspired Bach
unto more of his glorious musical compositions?
And needs must a spectre in these times
to inspire that much more to most people?

An Animal Abuse

An abused cat may not again
have so patent an existence-
A dog long-caged,
and finally released,
might run around in circles.
And the tenants of old age homes
might, too, be obliged in their course of stay
to be relieved
of some of their meaning of will.

Survival

In such a necessity
for survival,
or to draw the
superfluous consciousness out –
Or action is
the case
of either/or
in an animal's
what longstandingness.

Dogs and Cats

The scopic powers
of dogs and cats,
the subaltern group,
though, otherwise, silent:
The only thing
they still do
so remains
mostly powerless before us,
is to watch.

Spirit

Word

In gravitas, as quick as words can be
of the giving of information,
spirit is faster.
Therefore, the Word, or in the beginning,
may beget itself,
and if man-made,
the infiltration of the word from spirit,
or a silence,
could almost be predicable in the positive.

Words have changed
in their significance
from the 'creative'
in the ancient world
to 'agonistic'
in modernity.
Words, once a key of the focus,
but an adumbration, nowadays,
if less creative, and more like an 'awl' or a goad.

Words from the lexicon,
or implicitly beyond,
also, could be as henipoietic,
to suggest that
the origin of language
is a recollecting,
as humane,
or as supernormal,
in the less in being scientific.

Feud

199

Jewish relatives, not adults,
are still perennially pitched
in their agonism between
the consecutive charges of an 'emptiness',
or as an obstructing of an "aphanasia",
if having been as audacious,
still vis à vis the emptiness,
or a redemption is in the sufferable outcome
from the past, or onto this life.

aphanasia: darkness

The Rapture

America, becoming
a circumstance,
as a nation
of light
and in Christology,
or the present-day Jews,
with their
prior disavowal,
albeit is with their own Meschiach.

Intrinsic Idol

To be alone with oneself,
though there are people in the environs,
and a lack of necessary challenge, curiosity, or allegiance,
with which to work a matter out
in the community
and in oneself,
an allure,
that lickerish allure,
with its purpose:
Specifically, being the world's wound,
incarnate in the self,
with a modern nominality's
withdrawal of the sacred,
without, or within, to meddle with one's religiosity.

Ignorance

Ignorance is a sort of spirit's wandering,
that may precede
an evil impulse:
Not knowing
one's behavior's own swaggering repetition
to belie reason or understanding-
And a lack of a kind of divine presence
is that could burn through one,
before an illuminating of knowledge.

Empathy for a Dragging Sun

Is "non-over-again" a word?
I am subject to the arrow of time
and cannot altogether reverse myself,
nor can I bid always return to be a pert subject again,
a festering, but not in the tributaries of time:
For where is my purpose, as built,
to heal the wound?
Where is the solar spirituality?
Or could the sun, as well, drabble in these times?

Biography

Lee Goldstein was raised in Winnetka, near Chicago, and holds two master's degrees in technical fields, from Ann Arbor. In the early 1980's he worked in research and development in aerodynamics, at NASA. More recently, he has written for the small press, and is published in poetry, philosophy, and mathematics. He has one book of poetry, "Syntaxis', published (2002). Presently he resides in Lawrence, Kansas.